CHRIST IS THE LIGHT AND HOPE IN DARKNESS

Poems of Encouragement

R. L. TALLEY

PublishAmerica
Baltimore

© 2005 by R. L. Talley.
All rights reserved. No part of this book may be reproduced, stored in a retrieval system or transmitted in any form or by any means without the prior written permission of the publishers, except by a reviewer who may quote brief passages in a review to be printed in a newspaper, magazine or journal.

First printing

ISBN: 1-4137-6941-1
PUBLISHED BY PUBLISHAMERICA, LLLP
www.publishamerica.com
Baltimore

Printed in the United States of America

Contents

A TRIBUTE TO MY MOTHER   9
ACKNOWLEDGMENTS   11

LIFE SITUATIONS
    Are We to Judge   15
    Accept the Blame   18
    Lord, Do We Need You   20
    Hold Your Head Up   22
    I'm Tired   24
    Who Do We Honor   25
    What Are You Doing with Your Gift   26
    Wealth   27
    The Change in Man   29
    Clutter in Your Life   31
    Provider   34
    Are We Really Thankful   36
    Taking Blessings for Granted   38
    Looking Up to the Wrong One   40

BLACK HISTORY
    God Has Brought Us Through   45

NEW YEAR'S
Happy New Year   49
New Year's Greetings   51

CHRISTMAS
Holiday Greetings   55
Christmas Greetings   57
Truly Blessed   60
Christmas Past   61
Christmas New   62

THANKSGIVING
Remember to Give Thanks   65
Thanksgiving   66

DRUG ABUSE
What Would You Do   69
Crack Cocaine   71
Drugs Ruined My Life   73
Drugs, the Destroyer   75
Are You Any Better   77

ABUSE
We All Have Troubles   81
Why Did He   83
Rape   86
The Car Ride   88
I Blamed Him   90
Can They Feel My Pain   93
Take It Away   95
What Didn't I Do   97
The Assault   100
Party   102

Who Was the Abuser	104
Kinds of Abuse	106
Boyfriend	108
Company	110
Momma	112
The Practice	114

MOTHER
Who Is a Mother	119
A Godly Mother	123

RESURRECTION
He Arose	127
What He Did for Us	128

A Tribute to My Mother

I am blessed to have had two wonderful parents. Although I have very special and dear memories of my father, I dedicate this book to my precious mother, Mrs. Bessie Galloway, who went home to be with the LORD in June 2003. Mama always had faith in me. She would take my hands, smile at me, and always praise and encourage me for my efforts and thank GOD for giving her a "smart" daughter (her words, not mine). So again, with all of my love, I dedicate this book to my dear, sweet mother, whom I miss so much and will love forever.

I'm so grateful
That GOD made you my mom
And HE filled you with such motherly love
Mom, I'll see you again
When we meet in heaven above

For those who knew and loved you
You will live on in our hearts
Because of precious, precious memories
We will truly never be apart

Acknowledgments

First, I wish to acknowledge the power of the HOLY SPIRIT in giving me the insight to write these poems of encouragement to those who have suffered and are suffering various situations in their lives. I give thanks to the LORD because HE has brought me to this point and age in my life where I have not been touched by any of these heartbreaking circumstances.

At this time I would like to acknowledge and offer my deepest appreciation to those friends and co-workers who were gracious enough to give of their time, talent and patience to help, direct and encourage me in my efforts. I will list them in order of last name, not by type of help provided, because each part played was necessary and of vital importance. Linda Giles, Zenora Hines, Lauren Hughes, Shirley Machonis, Robert Norman, Kumar Radhakrisnan, Jeffrey Swartzbaugh, Eric Toatley and Deon Walker.

Guys, I know that it was a great test of your patience since my computer skills are pretty basic, so thanks again for all of your help and generosity in the sharing of your knowledge. Without you this would never have been. A huge thanks to those who encouraged me with their words and prayers. GOD bless each of you.

Love to my family: husband, Russell; son, Donald, and wife, Esther; daughter, Dianette; grandchildren, Alvin, Jr. and Rosie; step-daughter, Jacqueline; grandchildren, Pamela, Kevin, Samantha and Nicki. To siblings: Daniel; William and wife, Linda; Louis and wife,

Irma. To Aunt Ada, nieces, nephews and extended family. Sisters Mary and Bessie, who are at home with the LORD.

A heartfelt thanks to PublishAmerica for providing the opportunity for me to see the results of a dream come true. Thanks for considering my work worthy of publication.

With love and thanks,
R. L. Talley

Life Situations

ARE WE TO JUDGE

Do we really need to judge
Do we really have the right
To look upon another and say
That they walk in darkness, not in light

Are we really able and equipped
To know another's heart
Do our words and actions cause them
To be ridiculed and set apart

Do we really realize
How much damage we can cause
Before we put our mouths in motion
We should take a "mental" pause

There is none, no not one
Who is without some form of sin
At times we judge, on sin we see
Because we don't know the heart within

Sometime we judge each other
On the way we look, dress or talk
We need to accept each other with love
As we make this Christian walk

We may see a sister smoking
Play the lotto or have a drink
Before we start to gossip
We should stop and think

We don't know how far
That sister has come
With the LORD working with her along the way
We don't know what's she's been delivered from
And delivered from till this day

Maybe that drink is the "one a year"
That's she's worked down from "four a day"
Maybe that number, is the "one a month"
Instead of playing them "all" every day

Maybe that smoke is the "one a day"
Instead of a pack and a few
Maybe that sister is trying really hard
To be free of things like me and you

Because we only see the outer man
And not the man within
Because we judge on what we see
We should reflect upon where we've been

Maybe your idols are clothes, money, your job or a car
Or to be praised by men
If you put these things before GOD
That too is a sin

Are there things in your life
That CHRIST has brought you through
Pray for your sister, that through CHRIST
She will have the victory too

So if you see a sister is struggling
Don't be quick to put her down
Offer a kind word, a prayer, a hug
Don't look down on her with a frown

You may not smoke, gamble, or drink
Or you may hide your sin within
Remember that GOD knows our hearts
And to HIM, sin is sin

So let's be CHRISTLIKE in our hearts
And not be quick to condemn
CHRIST knows our faults and loves us still
Let's strive to be more like HIM

ACCEPT THE BLAME

The things that have happened in my life
And why my life is such a mess
I can't blame it on my folks
Because they did their very best

They taught me all about JESUS
And the road that I should travel
That lifestyle didn't offer much fun
So our closeness began to unravel

I wanted fun, sex and excitement
It seemed the Christian life was way too slow
I wanted to have a good time
I had things to do and places to go

I did whatever it took
To keep on having, what I thought was fun
But at the end of this party
I would pay for what I had done

I held jobs here and there
Long enough to save a little money
But I didn't take care of myself
And I started to look and feel real funny

I finally went to the doctor
And the report was pretty bad
AIDS was suspected
And AIDS is what I had

When my party friends found out
That I was sick and going to die
When I needed their comfort most
I couldn't find them, and I did try

My mom and dad are here for me
And JESUS never left my side
When I thought about how I hurt them and HIM
I hung my head and cried

I don't know how much time is left
But I'm using the time for gain
To tell men, women, boys and girls
That the blood of CHRIST washes away sin and stains

LORD, DO WE NEED YOU

LORD, do we need you
You know we really do
LORD, do we need you
There is no life without you

Daily each hour and minute
You allow us to breathe your precious air
Sometimes we take you for granted
Not giving a thought to how much you care

Where would we be without your blessings
How could we awake to a brand-new day
If YOU weren't so loving
Our lives would fade away

Do we take for granted the abilities
That you bestow upon us each day
We walk, talk, see and hear
And have a mind to go our way

We feel, love, pain and pleasure
We feel sorrow, loneliness and joy
We know grief, happiness and gratitude
We know and feel so much more

These are all a part of the mind and body
That only you could create
A being, man with all of his knowledge
Could never duplicate

Man's mind is the product of GOD's creation
That allows us to think, reason, learn and feel
Remember who is the giver of life
And know that our CREATOR lives, our CREATOR is real

HOLD YOUR HEAD UP

I was young, unmarried and pregnant
The father I didn't know
I had so many problems
I didn't know which way to go

I couldn't tell my parents
I couldn't tell my friends
I was living a nightmare
I didn't know when it would end

No one knows but me
About the new life that has begun
I was now in this situation
Because I thought having sex was having fun

The boy who I thought was the father
Denied it and left me alone
When I tried to see him or call his house
He would never come to the phone

I thought about abortion
Even though I knew it wasn't right
During the day I was in a trance
There was no sleep at night

I prayed and cried unto the LORD
LORD, please show me the way
I cannot carry this burden
I can't make it another day

The LORD was gracious unto me
And in HIS time made a way
HE gave me strength and courage
To face each brand-new day

My parents stood by me
They gave me much support and love
Although I didn't feel worthy
GOD continued to send blessings from above

I had a beautiful and healthy baby
Who brings me happiness each day
I've learned in all situations to trust in GOD
Because HE will always make a way

Even when we feel unworthy
And the world is looking dim
We must remember we are HIS children
And we are precious ones to HIM

I'M TIRED

I need your help, LORD
This hurt is too much for me
I come before you, LORD
I put my trust in thee

I'm tired and weak, LORD
From the hurt I carry each day
I come to you, LORD
Because YOU are the only way

Only you have the power, LORD
To restore my mind and soul
And I believe this, LORD
From all that I've read and been told

I stand in the need of a blessing, LORD
I need your healing power
I can't do it by myself, LORD
So I come to YOU this hour

To be free from this ache, LORD
I carry deep in my heart
Please show me what to do, LORD
And I will do my part

WHO DO WE HONOR

Who do we honor, who do we praise
Who do we thank, for all of our days

Who hears our troubles, who knows our cares
Who can we trust, who hears our prayers

Who never changes, who is always there
Who can we confide in, our secrets to share

Who is forgiving, who is a friend
Who will guide us, until the end

Who showers blessings, who gives us joy
Who knows all about, each man, woman, girl and boy

Who did all things on our behalf, who continues with us each day
Who holds our future in HIS hand, and leads us along the way

The answer my friend, is very clear
It's our LORD and SAVIOUR, ever near

JESUS CHRIST is HIS name
Yesterday, today and forever
HE's always the same

WHAT ARE YOU DOING WITH YOUR GIFT

Each of us has received a gift
The most precious gift of all
The gift of the SPIRIT and eternal life
If only on JESUS we would call

This gift was given to us
Wrapped in the body and blood of our LORD
To give us this special wrapping
HE was crucified and pierced with the sword

This gift we've been given, cost HIM no money
No long-term payments are due
JESUS paid the price in full
When on Calvary, HE died for me and you

This gift won't need to be exchanged
It doesn't come in color or size
Just believe that CHRIST, lived, died and was buried
And on Easter morn, HE did rise

To receive this gift is so simple
That's no shopping that you must do
Just repent, accept CHRIST as SAVIOUR
The gift is given immediately to you

We are to tell others how to receive the gift
By all that we say and do
HIS supply of gifts will never run out
There's one waiting for each of you

WEALTH

My baby wanted things
Fine clothes, a fine car and big house
When I said I couldn't afford it
She asked, "Are you a man or are you a mouse?"

Why can't I have nice things
And look and live like I want
If you can't provide these things
Why are we together, what's the point

Time passed so slowly
As we drifted further apart
What could I do to keep her
I loved her with all my heart

She withheld her body
She hurt me with her talk
If things didn't improve soon she said
She'd take a permanent walk

I prayed and prayed to GOD
To let my marriage last
To improve our relationship
And let this turmoil would soon pass

She suggested all kinds of things
To make quick and dirty money
I continued to pray to GOD
Because I really loved my honey

Something slowly happened to her
To cause her to stop seeking wealth
She had a new goal in life
To regain her failing health

Things are different now
She's like a different wife
She's come to realize
What's important in this life

No more abuse and threats
No more demand for material things
GOD has worked it out
Glory to the King of Kings

THE CHANGE IN MAN

What's going on in this world
Has man gone completely insane
Causing so much sorrow
Tears, grief and pain

Disregard for law and life
No thought for his fellow man
Just do whatever you need to do
To get all that you can

Rape, robbery, kidnapping and murder
Drugs, suicide and carjacking
Pornography, child abuse and school violence
What in their lives is lacking

JESUS is the answer
HE is the remedy for life's ills
Accept HIM as SAVIOUR
There would be no need for alcohol, drugs and pills

If man would only accept JESUS
And let HIM lead the way
And wait for JESUS to guide HIM
In all that he has to do and say

There would be a great change
In the way man handles daily problems and stress
He would go to the LORD in prayer
And let the FATHER take care of the rest

Man would begin to think of others
And try to live by the Golden Rule
But the love of CHRIST in their hearts
Would be the greatest tool

Change would come about
Through prayer and supplication
We would then be on the road again
To an "In GOD We Trust Nation"

CLUTTER IN YOUR LIFE

Is there clutter in your life
Is there disorder everywhere
Are there areas that need to be tidied up
Or have you reached the point where you just don't care

Are your heart and mind like overstuffed suitcases
Filled to the limit with cares and woes
You really don't need to take them along
But you lug the suitcases wherever you go

Family problems, lost love and friends
Maybe health problems and financial stress
They're crammed into the suitcase
On top of all the old mess

You continue to cram the suitcase
Never really dealing with the matters
You feel you can't put another thing in
You might lose your mind or your heart will shatter

At times you've talked things over with friends
Even confided in family, too
Either the problem never went away
Or it came back later to haunt you

There's only one solution to this situation
And HIS name is JESUS CHRIST
HE's the only one to help you
Keep your sanity and put some order into your life

Call on HIM, pray to HIM
Thank HIM and praise HIS name
Because yesterday, today and tomorrow
HE'll always be the same

HE knows our cares and worries
HE wants us to leave them with HIM
Because HE is the light
And shines brightest when things look dim

All the clutter, pain, mess and confusion
You lug around in your heart and mind each day
The weight and worry would be lifted
If these things on the altar you would lay

Will all the problems and cares vanish instantly
That's not for me to know
CHRIST is the only sustaining strength
And it's to HIM that we should go

Do you need strength and courage to live this life
With so many things going on
Remember that JESUS knows all that we would go through
HE knew it, even before we were born

HE selected you to be HIS heir
HE knows the road you would trod
HE wants you to trust HIM
Because we're HIS creation and HE's our GOD

There's no problem HE can't solve
HE hears our prayers when we pray
Trust in HIS timing and HIS solutions
And fellowship with HIM each day

So, the next time something comes your way
And you're tempted to cram again
Take your cares and woes to JESUS
HE loves you, HE's your GOD and HE's your FRIEND

THE PROVIDER

You're not a good provider
You fall short as a man
These are the words I hear
When I'm doing the best I can

When I wanted to go back to school
To make up the time that I lost
You tell me, "Don't even try it."
Keep both jobs at all cost

We need a vacation
We need to buy this or that
I now need a mink coat
To go with my new mink hat

I said that I would honor you
And cherish you as my wife
But things are going to be different
Since JESUS came into my life

I am the head of this family
JESUS ordained for me this place
Just as HE is the head
Of the entire human race

My love for you will continue
As GOD makes me the man HE wants me to be
I pray you remain by my side
And the changes you will see

In time things will work out
Just walk beside me, honey
And come to realize
There's more to life than just money

Caring, understanding, helping
Walking by my side with support and love
These are but a few of the things
That are required by GOD above

We'll become the family
That GOD envisioned from the start
Everything will work out
Keeping HIM in our minds and hearts

ARE WE REALLY THANKFUL

Are we just thankful
For the sun and not the rain
Are we only thankful
For the joy and not the pain

Are we only thankful
When prayers are answered in our favor
Do we in all situations
Give thanks unto our SAVIOUR

Are we thankful for our blessings
Both great and small
Are we thankful for what we have
Or do we want it all

There's a reason for the sunshine
And a reason for the rain
There's a reason for the joy
And a reason for the pain

These are all a part of life
And they help us all to grow
There's not a joy or pain we have
That our SAVIOUR doesn't know

Are we thankful for the sacrifice
That JESUS made for you and me
That we might have life
And have it more abundantly

That we should not perish
But have eternal life
So let us be thankful for
Our share of toil and strife

Let us show our LORD our gratitude
For all that HE did and does each day
By the life we live we show our thanks
For HIS blessings every day

LORD, we offer up to you
Our thanks and our praise
LORD, keep us close to YOU
For the rest of our days

When troubles come our way
And in the darkness we see no light
We know that some battles we may lose
But through YOU we'll win the fight

LORD, we thank you so much
For your love and your grace
LORD, keep us in your care
Until that day we see YOU face to face

TAKING BLESSINGS FOR GRANTED

Sometimes people take the blessings
GOD has so graciously given them
And go about their daily lives
Without ever acknowledging HIM

Some people take so much for granted
Even the air we breathe each day
We sometimes seem to think
That GOD has to send life our way

But take time to think
What would really take place
If GOD was to withdraw
HIS mercy, blessings and grace

The earth would cease to be
Mankind would be doomed to die
If GOD in HIS power didn't keep
HIS sun, moons, stars and planets held fast in the sky

What would we breathe
What would we eat
What would keep us from freezing
Or burning up in the heat

Who would control the seasons
And change day to night
No man or machine
Has that power or might

So always give GOD thanks
Each and every day
Thank HIM for HIS blessings
That HE sends our way

Never take for granted
All the blessings that GOD daily gives
It's only HIS power that keeps us
And because of that we know our SAVIOUR lives

LOOKING UP TO THE WRONG ONE

Did you ever put your trust in someone
And that person let you down
Your spirits were so low
You felt your chin was dragging the ground

You admired them, you looked up to them
You thought that their lives were first rate
You envied them, you applauded them
You thought that person was simply great

Then rumors started surfacing about them
The terrible things they said couldn't be true
Molestation, rape, drugs, adultery, lying and stealing
Things my idol just wouldn't do

You dismissed everything as lies
You said jealousy was the reason for it all
These were movie stars, athletes, entertainers
Even men who had answered GOD's call

Its easy sometime to get caught up
And admire people for their glamour and worth
But you must remember none of this will go with you
When you leave this earth

Don't look at wealth or fame, but
Look at peoples lives and see
If they have accepted CHRIST as KING
Because CHRIST is who's important
When you strip away material things

Things can come and go
In the blink of an eye
But when you accept CHRIST
HE will be with you till you die

It's okay to look at people
And admire them for the rough road they may have trod
But remember they wouldn't have made it at all
But for the grace and mercy of GOD

To have HIM as your LORD and SAVIOUR
Is worth more than silver, gold and fame
Because GOD will give you needed blessings
Many more than you can name

Blessings aren't always material
There are many things money can't do
Just be grateful and blessed and know
That you have a powerful GOD who loves you

There's no idol you should have
JESUS is the one to be worshipped and lifted up
Because JESUS is the one who blesses us
HIS blessings overflow our cup

Black History

GOD HAS BROUGHT US THROUGH

We've had a lot of struggles
We've endured a lot of pain
We held fast and didn't give up
We had too much to gain

We were taken from our homeland
We were hurt, but we had to stay strong
We were led by GOD's hand
Even though we suffered long

From fields of cotton with overseers
And the big house on the plantation
They couldn't kill our spirit nor our will
We were part of GOD's blessed creation

They separated our families
Dishonored and abused our ancestral sisters and mothers
They tried to break the hearts, minds, bodies and spirits
Of our ancestral fathers and brothers

But we survived the pain each day
We endured the tears and sorrow
We held hope within our hearts and prayed
Because we knew that GOD held tomorrow

GOD kept us looking up
When troubles came our way
HE strengthened us every morning
To face a brand-new day

We've come a long way together
We've accomplished a lot of great things
We're thankful as a race
That we heard the bells of freedom ring

There are so many great things that we've done
That we don't get credit for
But we can't let that stop us
We must continue to do more and more

We must never forget our past nor our forefathers
The shed blood and all they went through
They struggled and kept the faith
To make a better life for me and you

Prejudice, hatred and racism come
With many different faces
Because of your faith, age or sex
And often because of your race

We're hated for the color of our skin
When we should accepted for what's in the heart
When the skin is stripped away
We're all the same, you can't tell us apart

Don't lose the ground we've gained
Don't ease backward, forge ahead
Don't get comfortable and think everything is okay
Racism and prejudice are a long way from being dead

So take pride in yourself and accomplish
Positive things for GOD, yourself and your race
We are where we are today
Because of GOD's Mercy and HIS Grace

New Year's

HAPPY NEW YEAR

The old year might have brought
A variety of happenings into your life
Some brought joy and satisfaction
Others brought pain and strife

Death, sickness, pain and sorrow
Touched our lives or touched someone we knew
Disappointment, failure, tears that flowed
Must have had their share too

But, through the year it wasn't all bad
There were days of happiness and fulfillment too
We knew that whatever occurred
GOD would see us through

We may have been in the midst of many storms
And felt we couldn't ride out the storm anymore
But we remained steadfast and faithful in prayer and
HE brought us through and placed us safely on the shore

We sent up prayers, for various reasons
Some were answered, but not always in the time or way we felt was best
We must give our burdens to HIM, that's our part
And let HIM in HIS wisdom do the rest

We had times of laughter, healing and success,
Victory and answered prayer
We remembered to go to HIM and HIS WORD
Because we know that HE really cares

We've been saved and strengthened
And kept by HIS grace
Only through the power of GOD
Can we win this race

We remembered to give HIM thanks
And to praise HIS holy name
Because we know; yesterday, today and tomorrow
HE remains the same

Whatever the new year may bring
Remember to go to HIM to rest
Because as children of GOD we can't have
A testimony without a test

Remember GOD is with us, not against us
He's with us every day
Lean on HIM, talk to HIM
Ask HIM to show you the way

Rely on HIS Word,
Lean on HIS arms
Let HIM your burdens bear
Because we know HE loves us
And that HE really cares

NEW YEAR'S GREETINGS

HE was with us in the sunshine
HE brought us through the rain
HE was with us in joyful times
HE brought us through the pain

HE kept us through uncertain times
HE was with us in our grief
We were able to keep our joy
When the enemy came as a thief

HE made a way when the money was short
HE was with us when bills were long
HE was with us when we were weak
HE was with us and kept us strong

HE was a friend when we were lonely
HE was a doctor when illness came
I thank GOD that JESUS is never changing
I'm thankful that HE remains the same

The year may have had its share
Of problems, stress and strain
But thank GOD we made it through
It was something that HE had ordained

The year had its losses
The year had its gains
The year had its laughter
The year had its pains

The year has some success
It had some failures too
It had some things that fell apart
And others that held true

But looking back over it
There's only one thing to say
Thank GOD that HE brought us through
To another year and a brand-new day

We thank GOD for all of our blessings
We thank GOD for all that HE's done4
We thank GOD and the HOLY SPIRIT
And JESUS CHRIST THE SON

Christmas

HOLIDAY GREETINGS

Before we wish you greetings
Of the holiday season
We want to give you something to think of
And this is the reason

With all the money in the world
And all the brilliant minds
Why can't we get together
And do something for mankind

The poverty and disease
The suffering and the strife
Why can't things be done
To make it a better life

It seems to me, with all our wealth
This country could do something
To improve our minds and health

The many people starving
And the many with no place to live
Why don't they that are more fortunate
Open up their hearts and give

Some of us are wealthy
And some of us don't have as much as we want
But this is what I'm trying to convey
And here is the point

Christ is the guest of honor
    And it's HIS birthday we're celebrating this season
Help those less fortunate
    And this is the reason
Riches and good health
    Are just a few reasons to send thanks above
Interest and a will to help
    Are things, which we need a lot more of
Seeing and reading of the crime, the war
    And the terrible things happening each day
Things like that should make us thankful and want to help
    So that nothing like that will come directly our way
Make each day count, each minute and hour
    Try to help your fellow man
    Try to spread a little happiness
    Into each life that you can
Always answer when the needs call
    Don't be afraid to lend a helping hand
    Because of all the people in the world
    We're just like little grains of sand
So it matters a lot if we stand alone, or if we group together
    Because a mountain of us together can withstand the changes of weather
    So Merry Christmas and have a Happy New Year
    And may you always walk in joy and peace in life
    May you never have to learn to live in suffering and strife

I believe that God intended for us
To love and help each other
And for each man to live and treat
The next man as a brother

Brothers have their fallings out
They curse and rant and rave
But to get this sad world straighten out
Is a road we, ourselves, have to pave

CHRISTMAS GREETINGS

Hustle and bustle
To and fro
Where did all of
The time and money go

Mornings, evenings
Weekends, too
Go, go, go
So much to do

Did I get the colors
And the sizes right
Or as soon as I leave
Will the gift be put out of sight

Is the gift useful
Or was it just a waste
Did I mail the correct package
To the right place

Slow down, slow down
Quit the rush
As always, during this time
You try to do too much

Shopping and cooking
Traveling all over town
Take care of yourself
Rest, settle down

The giving of gifts
Is a nice thing to do
The spirit behind the giving
Lies within you

Was it given to impress
Or make a grand show
Was it given out of love
That's something only you know

Do we give of ourselves all year
Do we offer smiles and a warm hello
Or are we so wrapped up in our lives
That others seem invisible wherever we go

Some gifts we can give cost no money
They suit all colors, sizes and tastes
We can give them over and over
These gifts never go to waste

Without HIS birth
Men would be forever lost
So celebrate JESUS
For this there is no cost

Share the gift of the love of JESUS CHRIST
Tell the Good News to all men
Let others know of salvation
And how they must be born again

Visit the sick, feed the hungry, clothe the naked,
Lift up those who are feeling low
Tell men what a FRIEND we have in JESUS
Tell it to all men, wherever you go

Give your gifts of love to family and friends
And enjoy this Blessed Season
In all you do, in all you say
Remember – JESUS is the Reason

TRULY BLESSED

Hello, Merry Christmas
And have a Happy New Year
May you live to raise your glass
In many a toast of cheer

As we rush back and forth
Trying to get last minute details done
So that on Christmas Day, we can relax
Sit back and start to have some fun

Don't forget to thank HIM
For letting us these pleasant times enjoy
For it's through HIM that we receive our blessings
From the oldest man or woman
To the youngest girl or boy

Sometimes we don't realize
How blessed we really are
That we can walk down the street
Until we come upon someone
Who has no legs or feet

There are many other things
Too numerous, that I could say
To make us more aware
Of how blessed we are today

Count your blessings
All that comes your way
Things may get tough sometimes
But thank GOD it's not tough every day

CHRISTMAS PAST

A time for little token gifts
Of our gratefulness and love
And a time to give special thanks
For our blessings from above

Showing kindness and appreciation for others
Throughout the entire year
Trying to help others and make them happy
Which makes memories we can hold dear

Making a call, dropping a note
Or stopping by once in a while
Are things we can do year round
And perhaps cause someone to smile

CHRISTMAS NEW

Going out and buying
The most expensive gifts we can
Maybe trying to impress others
Be it child, woman or man

Taking one day out of the year
To put on a show we may not mean
By trying to be the most generous person
That anyone's ever seen

Sending out cards by the dozen
With a name and not much more
In hopes that the return mail
Will bring many back to your door

The Spirit of Christmas past
Or the Spirit of Christmas new
Look deep within yourself and decide
Which is the spirit for you

So let's take time to think about it
And remember what Christmas means
Reflect upon the moment in time
And the meaning of the Christmas theme

It's time to renew a way of life that
We should carry throughout the days
To live and care for our brothers
Not only in big, but in little ways

Thanksgiving

REMEMBER TO GIVE THANKS

Well, tomorrow is the day
For which some of us have planned all year
Some of us have invited guest and relatives
From far and near

We knocked down the turkey population
By quite a few
We'll be using old recipes
And experimenting with the new

We'll sit down to a table
Loaded with a lot of good things
We'll carve a turkey and then decide
Who'll get the drumstick or the wing

But before we dig in
And start to chow
We should remember to give thanks
And this is how

Fold your hands
And bow your head
And thank the LORD
For your daily bread

Thank HIM for HIS goodness
And the blessings HE has sent
Thank HIM for blessings, great and small
While your heart is humble and your head is bent

THANKSGIVING

The fourth Thursday in November
Is upon us once more
When relatives and friends
Will come knocking at your door

When your table is set
With all the tasty treats
From the soup or salad
To the tempting meats

But there's one thing I think
That is eluding us more each year
And that is why, this holiday is one
That we should hold especially dear

We experience a lot of things in life
Some events we wish to forget
And others we want to remember
But let us never forget the meaning of
The fourth Thursday in November

Be thankful that GOD has let us live
And endure all that we have been through
Life hasn't been all roses for me
As I'm sure it hasn't been for you

So give extra thanks on Thanksgiving
For your blessings both great and small
For GOD knows and cares about us
And hears our prayers, when on HIM we call

Drug Abuse

WHAT WOULD YOU DO

How much would you do
Beg, borrow or steal
Would you go so far
As to maybe even kill

Would it bother you at all
To take someone's life
Be it someone's husband, son or father
Someone's daughter, mother or wife

When you're craving your drugs
Nothing has value to you
You'll do whatever it takes
To feed the drug demon inside of you

You'll sell your possessions
Lose loved ones, jobs, home and friends
You'll shoplift, prostitute and lie
And cause relationships to end

At times you may feel sorry
And look back and have regret
But that won't last long
Because the demon has a hunger to be met

You may get to the point and say
There is no hope for me
I'm lost, I'm down, I've hurt and cried
There's no way out that I can see

Don't give up, get up, look up
Ask JESUS CHRIST to make a way
It may seem dark and gloomy as night
But JESUS can make it seem like a new day

Go to HIM, surrender to HIM
Let HIM mold you just like clay
Learn of HIM, pray to HIM
Walk with HIM each day

Just stay with HIM and learn
HE will put and keep you on the right track
Once you accept CHRIST as SAVIOUR
Follow HIM, there'll be no going back

But you must be sincere
When asking HIM to guard your heart
You must have faith and trust in HIM
That's just doing your part

There'll be hurts to be healed
There'll be wrongs to be made right
Just be patient and let GOD work it out
It won't happen overnight

CRACK COCAINE

Crack cocaine was my drug of choice
It was cheap and a quick thrill
It didn't matter to me then
That a tiny rock had the power to kill

Death comes in many ways
And death stops many things
Crack cocaine brings pain and sorrow
Before the final death it brings

Lost hope, lost love
Lost dreams and lost life
It can destroy relationships
And bring nothing but hurt and strife

It doesn't matter how it started
In only matters that it can end
You can have victory over crack
Accept JESUS as SAVIOUR and FRIEND

The road may not be easy
To overcome this enemy in your life
You cannot achieve the victory
Without JESUS CHRIST

There is a rock for you
A rock full of power, love and grace
JESUS CHRIST is the rock
The SAVIOUR of the human race

So make a trade in your life
Get rid of the rock that can kill
Accept JESUS CHRIST as LORD
HIS love for you will be your greatest thrill

Life won't be smooth and easy
You'll have knocks and bumps along the way
Let JESUS be your companion
HE will direct your path each day

When the victory has been won
Always give thanks to JESUS CHRIST the son

DRUGS RUINED MY LIFE

It's all my doing
I thought drugs were cool
They've ruined my life
Now who's the fool

I thought I could handle it
I could keep it under control
By my life ended up as a play
And drugs had the starring role

My life had become a real tragedy
It was full of hurt, depression and pain
There was so much that was wrong
Would my life be worth living again

My marriage is nearly over
I've lost my friends
My kids disown me
Will this nightmare ever end

I'd tried a few times before
To get my life back on track
But as soon as anything went wrong
The lure of drugs called me back

I was weak ashamed and tired
I felt that no good would come of my life
But I finally gave in to her pleading
And went to a church service with my wife

I had put the family through hell
But their love for me was still there
I felt so unworthy
I wondered how they could still care

The words were powerful and painful
And it seemed as if he preached just to me
But the words gave me hope
That from drugs I could be set free

I continued under the word
And soon accepted JESUS as the head of my life
The way hasn't been easy
But now I turn to JESUS in times of strife

The battle is being fought as I live
Day out and day in
As long as I hold to JESUS
The battle I will win

DRUGS, THE DESTROYER

Drugs, drugs, drugs
It's always more, more, more
It doesn't take much to get started
But your life they can destroy

Nothing will have much worth
Nothing but getting the drugs will matter
All of your hopes and dreams
The use of drugs will shatter

There are all kinds of drugs
That can so easily get you hooked
Over the counter, prescription
Inhaled, injected, smoked or cooked

The addiction serves only one purpose
That is to destroy, degrade and kill
Once you are addicted
The drugs have you at their will

You don't have the strength to stop
Because you are too weak
You need to pray to JESUS
It's HIS help you should seek

Ask HIM for forgiveness
Ask HIM to wash you clean
Let HIM guide your life
And on HIS strength you have to lean

HE's mightier than the addiction
HE's truer than you can know
Accept HIM as your way-maker
And always to HIM you should go

There may be days
When it looks bad
You may feel defeated
And feel so sad
Don't give up, hang in there

JESUS loves you, JESUS cares

ARE YOU ANY BETTER

Because you're not doing illegal drugs
Smoking marijuana or smoking crack
You don't feel or really think
That you don't have a drug demon on your back

What about the empty liquor bottles
Hidden all around the house
What about sneaking and drinking alone
Trying to be quiet as a mouse

What about the many times
When you drink till you're passed out
How many times did you say "no more"
If I can just get over this bout

How many times were you drunk
When you drove the car
And woke up the next day
Not remembering how you got this far

Things are so hazy and your head is fuzzy
You can't remember which road you traveled
You begin to feel shaky and sick to your stomach
And now your nerves begin to unravel

You wonder, did I hit anyone
Did I cause any harm
You really can't remember
And you become quite alarmed

You feel you don't have a drug problem
Though you've had blackouts before
You feel it can't be a drug problem
Because you "bought" your liquor from a store

You can't keep doing what you're doing
You won't keep getting by
One day your drinking will kill you
Or cause someone else to die

You tried on your own
To get rid of the need to drink
You knew you couldn't do it
You just had to think, think, think

But after all the ways you tried
To get and stay sober and clean
You found that you were too weak
You needed on someone stronger to lean

It took some time and doing
Mistakes were made and falls happened along the way
You fell but didn't stay down
JESUS was there to help you along the way

No, it wasn't easy
And you didn't overcome drinking overnight
You had to keep faith in JESUS
And keep HIS path in your sight

You're still following HIM
And trusting HIM along the way
To remain victorious in battle
It's with JESUS you heart must stay

Abuse

WE ALL HAVE TROUBLES

Why do some people
Always seem so happy
And others always seem to be stressed
How can there be such a difference
When we as GOD's children are all blessed

We all have trouble in this life
Or a painful past that's a burden to bear
We keep things hidden and bury them deep
Because we wonder if anyone cares

Sometimes behind that smiling face
There are troubles, cares and woe
The difference between the smile and frowning face
Is knowing where with your problems you should go

Do you go to friends and family
Can they solve all the problems
That come your way
The only trouble with that is this
Friends and family are not here to stay

The minute you need one of them
Some may be too busy or not around
Sometime if they know a problem is coming
They most definitely don't want to be found

There is someone who listens
And HIS advice will never cause you to fall
HE is omnipresent, so
HE's there whenever you call

Take your burdens to CHRIST JESUS
Trust HIM to always be there
HE will never leave you nor deceive you
Because HE loves you and HE does cares

WHY DID HE

I trusted my uncle
He was always a lot of fun
He said I didn't seem like a nephew
I seemed more like a son

I remember when I was little
We had fun playing games
But when I got older
The playing wasn't the same

He assured me there was no harm
In the things he made me do
But he always told me to tell no one
He said, "It's a secret between me and you."

I didn't like the things he did
Or the way that made me feel
At those times, I'd hope I was dreaming
But I knew it was all too real

I wanted to tell my mother
I wanted to tell my father
My uncle said they wouldn't believe you
So why even bother

I kept the dirty secret
Until my family moved away
But the scars it made on my life
Are with me every day

When my uncle died, I felt no sorrow
Just joy that he was dead
I would never have to think about
Him crawling in another child's bed

The secrets of those terrible years
Are buried deep in my heart
When he died I felt relief
A brand-new life I could start

But it wasn't that easy
Because I continued to carry the hate
Now that he's dead, the pain will go away
I'll have to be patient and wait

I'm grown and married now
With a family of my own
I thought it would be over by now
But the hate hasn't gone

As I sat in Sunday service
With my friends and family on the pew
I often wonder what the people would think
If they only knew

How much hatred I carried within
For something that happened years ago
My uncle was dead and gone
And no one would ever know

The HOLY SPIRIT had been working
Over the years to let me know
That this hatred that I carried
Could not stay, it had to go

It is not of GOD to hate
It is of GOD to forgive
This change had to happen
If for CHRIST I wanted to live

So sitting on that pew
With loved ones all around
I went to GOD in prayer
Only through HIM could healing be found

It didn't happen overnight
But I feel the changes in my heart
When you seek healing and restoration
It's with JESUS you should start

RAPE

Do you have those painful memories
From so many years past
You felt so guilty and defiled
You didn't want your life to last

The late-night trips into your bedroom
When others were asleep
When a large hand covered your mouth
So you wouldn't make a peep

The probing hands upon your breast
The rough hands upon your hips
The weight upon your small body
The kiss upon your lips

You laid there and suffered the abuse
During many a night
You were warned to tell no one
You were to keep your mouth shut tight

In the morning when you arose
And tried to wash the filth away
Your pain and shame were so heavy
How could you make it through the day

Who could you tell
Of the things going on
Who would believe you
Would they say that you were wrong

Would they say you were dreaming
And had a bad nightmare
Who could you tell
You needed someone to care

Those nights are over now
You lived through all those years
No one will ever know the pain
Or the reason for so many tears

You are a survivor
And there is someone who cares
HIS name is JESUS CHRIST
And HE hears you through your prayers

No one can turn back the clock
And take the hurt away
But take your pain to the LORD
And with HIM let it stay

Time is a good healer
For the body and the mind
But JESUS is the Greatest Healer
HE's the Creator of mankind

THE CAR RIDE

The speedometer neared ninety
It seemed as if the car would really fly
I didn't know that very soon
There would be pain, death and tears to cry

We were out having a good time
As we did every Saturday night
I drove the car while I was high
Even though I knew it wasn't right

Where did that car come from
I can't stop; we're going to crash
The last thing I remember was my body
Going through the glass

I woke up days later
I was in the hospital and in great pain
But the greatest hurt was finding out
I would never see my friends again

Even though the other car was at fault
Because he had run the red light
I too had to pay for my part
In causing my friends death that night

Maybe it wouldn't have happened
If I hadn't been driving high
All I knew was that I had a part
In causing my friends to die

I spent time in prison
I was raped and abused while there
My only thought was of what I had done
So I really didn't care

I'm back on the street now
Drugs and alcohol are my friends
I know that I must suffer
And I didn't want my suffering to end

Many people prayed to GOD for me
I didn't want to hear what they had to say
I had created my own hell
And in this hell I deserved to stay

For those who were praying for me
The prayers made a breakthrough
If prayer could make a change in my life
They can do the same for you

Each day is getting just a little easier
To live without the guilt and pain
Thanks to JESUS who answers prayers
And washed away my guilty stain

I BLAMED HIM

My older brother had a party
While Mom and Dad were away
What happened to me that night
I haven't forgiven him for till this day

He and his friends were laughing
All the guys and girls were having fun
I sat on the stairs and watched them
Saying I'll sleep when this party's done

It seemed the party would never end
I got tired and went to bed
A hand over my mouth awakened me
And this is what the voice said

If you ever tell anyone
What I'm about to do
I'll come back and kill your family
And I'll make you watch before I kill you

I was terrified and sick
I couldn't stop the tears
The horrible things he did to me
Were worse than any I feared

It seemed like an eternity
Before he left me in so much pain
I lay there crying and praying
Please don't let him come back again

I cried, I cried, I cried
How could I tell anyone
I hated my brother because
While I suffered, he was having fun

The years passed by slowly
In my heart I held hate and pain
I never told my brother
And it never happened again

My life was such a mess
I was a Christian but I carried hate
I knew that hate was not of GOD
I had to reconcile before it was too late

My brother asked how I could live like this
And let my hatred for him grow
He asked why didn't I tell him
How else was he to know

He said if only I had told him
So that he could have tried to set things straight
He wanted to know how I could live a life
Filled with so much pain and hate

I confessed to my brother
That the blame was mine too
I was so scared
I didn't know what to do

It was easier to blame him
Than to let others know my shame
And wonder if they would believe me
Since I didn't know the boy's name

I asked my brother to forgive me
For the years we lost
I asked God to forgive
for what my hatred had cost

My brother and I have reconciled
I know that this pleases the LORD
After all the pain and all the blame
We're now on one accord

CAN THEY FEEL MY PAIN

Friends sometimes seem to care
As you tell them of your painful past
Of the rape, abuse and maybe incest
But how long does their caring last

Some say they can imagine
But if they didn't live it, how would they know
Of the hurt and nightmarish memories
That are with you wherever you go

Not being able to feel free
To live the life that I want
Always afraid something will trigger the hurt
So I say to myself, what's the point

I tried to make myself content
And live life from day to day
I had no joy, until a friend asked
Have you accepted CHRIST, because HE is the way

HIS power to restore is beyond all belief
We are HIS children and HE wants us to know
Don't keep taking your problems anywhere else
First to the LORD in prayer you should go

No it wasn't easy
To leave my hurts at the altar
And not take them away
It was a process I had to learn
Because it was at the altar
That my cares had to stay

Finally, I was on the right path
To a whole new way to live
Now I go to HIM in prayer
And to HIM my burdens I give

TAKE IT AWAY

Do you really feel better
Or do you think that you do
After all of the horrible things
That you had happen to you

Was it incest or rape
Or physical abuse that happened so long ago
Things that were so painful
You never want anyone to know

Were you young and innocent
And just beginning to live
When this horror came your way
Did it hurt so much and scar you so much
You still carry the pain to this day

Did you feel that no one could ever understand
The degrading things that happened to you
Did you feel that if others found out
There would be talk, stares and gossip too

You put on a good front to mask your hurt
You go through life hiding your pain
You keep all the horror to yourself
By telling others you have nothing to gain

There is someone waiting for you
To come to HIM in prayer
HE's waiting for you to give HIM your pain
HE's waiting HE really does care

Tell HIM the hurt that you carry each day
Tell HIM it's gotten too heavy to bear
Ask HIM to take the pain away
HE's waiting, HE loves you, HE cares

Wait on the LORD to lift your burden
And take the pain away
But you must trust HIM and be patient
HE works in HIS own time and in HIS own way

WHAT DIDN'T I DO

I went to bed early
To get some needed rest
I tried to get to sleep
I tried my very best

After hours of tossing and turning
I saw the first rays of light
I asked myself, how did you
Make it through the night

So many problems
So many loose ends
I'm too ashamed
To talk to my friends

They may wonder how a child of GOD
Got herself into this mess
So I won't bother them
I'll work it out; I'll do my best

I don't want anyone to know
For fear of judgment and talk
They might wonder, is she
On the path GOD would have her walk

Is she paying her tithe
Is she praying and fasting
Is she doing the works
That will remain everlasting

Is she attending church services
And doing her part
Is she serving the LORD
With a joyful heart

Is she witnessing and telling others
Of the way to eternal life
If she's doing all this
Then why so much strife

Does she treat those in the body of CHRIST
With the love of the LORD
Do strangers receive help when needed
Or are they just ignored

I ask myself repeatedly
Why am I struggling so much
Have I done something wrong
Have I lost the LORD's fixing touch

Seems that others all around me
Are enjoying blessings and GOD's grace
While it appears that from me
GOD has hidden His face

New bills, overdue bills, sickness
Job and family problems too
I finally turned to the LORD
And asked LORD what must I do

It's time to turn it over to the LORD
I tried and gave it my best
This is the peace that came over me
And put my mind at rest

Tell the LORD all about it
Everything that's troubling you
These are the things that I was led to do

Don't be concerned with other's blessings
You don't know the reason or the story
Keep you faith in the LORD at all times
And continue to give HIM glory

Pray more, read the WORD more
Study and stay in prayer
Continue to praise and thank the LORD
No matter what your burdens or cares

Instead of dwelling on your troubles
And thinking of all of your woes
Think of God and all of HIS blessings
And see how quickly your worries go

The LORD is on your side
And in HIS time HE will see you through
Continue to have faith and patience
Trust that HE loves you, HE knows and cares
That's all you have to do

THE ASSAULT

I thought I'd take a shortcut
To get home quicker that night
I didn't realize
There would be so little light

The path became deserted
I'd come too far to turn around
I thought mine were the only footsteps
Till I heard another sound

Maybe it was an animal
Scurrying into the night
I began to experience
The beginnings of fright

I quickened my pace
Without looking around
The next thing I knew
I was thrown to the ground

A gun was placed
Beside my head
If I said a word
I would soon be dead

The assault took place
There in the dark
Why did I even
Walk through that park

I told no one
I felt so low
I often wondered
Did my feelings show

I carried the pain and guilt
For a very long time
Until I finally told
A close friend of mine

I told her it was my fault
For taking the path that night
She said we all make mistakes
Only JESUS' judgment is always right

No matter how old the attack
Reminders always surface from your past
Come to JESUS seeking a healing
For HIS healing will last and last

HE is the Creator
And knows our suffering and pain
Only HE can cleanse our spirits
And make us whole again

PARTY

My beau asked me to the party
He said it would be very nice
If I had only known then
I wouldn't now have to pay this price

It was a very nice party
Everything was going fine
Until I found in the next room
They were doing drugs and drinking wine

My head began to twirl
As I smelled the sweet smoke
My eyes began to water
I coughed and began to choke

I shouldn't feel this way
I began to think
Had anyone put a drug
In the soda that I had to drink

Things that happened after that
Have never been real clear
I seemed to be in a fog
I could barely walk, talk, see or hear

Nobody confessed to know
Who slept with me that night
They said whoever did it
It certainly wasn't right

My date said it wasn't him
He wouldn't do such a thing
A few months later, we split
And he took back his ring

Time has passed very slowly
The baby is due any day
I have decided to keep the baby
And not give him away

I've had my share of scorn
But I held my head up high
Because I now have a SAVIOUR
With a home beyond the sky

GOD will lead me on the path
And the road that I should take
HE will guide me as what to do
For HIS and this baby's sake

WHO WAS THE ABUSER

Did he slap you
Did he kick you
Did he rape you
Night after night

Did she kiss you
Did she touch you
Did she make you do
What wasn't right

Was it Mother, was it Father
Was it a stranger, or a friend
In your mind did you wonder
Will this nightmare ever end

All those terrible feelings
All the guilt and the shame
How would you ever
Feel clean and decent again

You look back at the years
And almost daily relive the pain
The hurt and hatred that you feel
Won't come out, they're like a stubborn stain

No matter what you do
To drive the pain and memories away
Something triggers the memory
And the hurt comes back to stay

Only JESUS knows your suffering
HE knows exactly how you feel
Only JESUS can bring you healing
Because HE knows your pain is real

Only JESUS is mighty enough
To restore body, heart and mind
HE's the only one who can heal you
JESUS is one of a blessed kind

HE'll heal your abused body
HE'll renew your mind and thoughts
Go quickly to JESUS, the Great Physician
HIS restoration is free, it can't be bought

KINDS OF ABUSE

There are so many ways
To bring about abuse
From the way we talk
To the drugs we use

We abuse with our hands
And with the words we say
Abuse is so painful
Only GOD can take the pain away

The harm we do
To ourselves and each other
No one is immune
Mother, father, sister or brother

There's physical, mental and verbal abuse
Child abuse, sexual and elder abuse too
When we read of the types of pain inflicted
We ask can that horror really be true

Some of us may have a painful past
We may feel the hurt will last and last
But give it to JESUS, to HIM daily prayer
In time HE'll heal mind and body
And take the pain away

Give your pain and hurt to JESUS
Ask forgiveness for your hate
Go to JESUS to be comforted
Go now, it's not too late

Pray for the one who abused you
Ask JESUS to help you mend
Go to JESUS for a healing
HE's your Father and HE's your friend

BOYFRIEND

He was my boyfriend
And I thought our love was true
Until there were things
That he asked me to do

Our bills were overdue
And our rent was way behind
He said there's a way you can help
If you love me, you won't mind

He had lost his job
And my pay was very low
He said, "I have the answer
This is the way to go."

You have a fine body
And a pretty face
Just go on a few dates
And I know just the place

I asked him if he was crazy
Wanting me to sell my body that way
He said if I didn't do it
There was no way he was going to stay

I asked him about his love for me
And how he could ask me to such a thing
He said that as soon as we're on our feet
You'll finally get that ring

Many times I went out
And sold my body for that man
I told him it wasn't right
I couldn't make him understand

Through all the times I was out there
Our bills were still behind
But I did notice now
That he was beginning to dress real fine

I thought what I felt for him
Was genuine caring and love
I was out there doing as he had asked
Then came intervention from above

As soon as I got to the corner
There was a group from the local church
They were there seeking others for JESUS
And I ended up in their search

They told me the Good News of JESUS
That I didn't have to live this way
My life has been changed forever
Since that blessed day

I still go to that corner regularly
But I'm in a different frame of mind
I pass out tracts and spread the Good News
It's JESUS you need to find

COMPANY

Men may wonder why
I rebuke their advances
I don't allow too many men
To have very many chances

I like the company of men
There are nice places I like to go
Museums, dinner, cycling
On a picnic or take in a show

Holding hands, a gentle kiss
A hug, a warm embrace
I wonder can they see the pain
Behind the smile that's on my face

I'll never give them a chance
To get too serious about us
I find a reason to end the relationship
And I do it with little fuss

It really pains me for this to happen
Over and over again
I can never allow a man
To become more than just a friend

They'll never know what happened
That caused me to be this way
How I truly loved a man
Who used me and tossed me away

The doctors and pills didn't help
The pain and scars were very deep
I toss and turn at night
Trying to get some sleep

I want to trust again
I want a husband in my life
A man who will cherish me
And honor me as his wife

I now know there's only one way
To recover from this pain
That's to put JESUS as the head
Of my soul and life again

HE'll do the counseling and healing
And help me recover what was lost
I need only to go to HIM
And leave my burdens at the cross

HE'll bring a mate my way
If that's HIS heavenly will
Until and if that happens
My soul says "peace be still"

MOMMA

Oh, Momma
Why didn't you see the signs
That things weren't right
Or were you too busy
Going out, night after night

I was too young to explain
What was happening to me
I was hoping that you would
Take the time to look and really see

Didn't you see me flinch
When you washed me down below
Didn't you notice the scratches
Or didn't you want to know

Did you stop and wonder why
I cried whenever he entered my sight
When other men came around
I seemed to be all right

You never checked his past
To see if he had problems before
He was abusing me
Almost before you shut the door

Thank GOD the meeting was cancelled
And you came home earlier than he thought
Thank GOD you came into the room
Now at last he has been caught

He was tried and sent to jail
You thought it was over and done
You chose a woman to watch me now
A new madness has just begun

So, Mother, PLEASE pray for me
Ask GOD to protect me every day
I can think and I can feel
But I'm too young to have a say

You have to pray for me
You have to pray every day
So that GOD can send the angels
And around me they will stay

THE PRACTICE

After-school practice
Nearly every day
Slowly the other kids
Have gone on their way

Why so much practice
Why am I the only one
Things are starting to happen
This is no longer fun

Why does the coach need to be
So close to show me the right way
Why does he have to be so close
When he has something to say

Why do his hands and body
Have to touch me so much
Doesn't he know I don't like it
When he finds a reason to touch

When I finally spoke to him
And said I was getting off the team
He said, if you tell anybody
I'll make an end to your dreams

Who would believe you anyhow
That I would do such a thing to you
And what proof do you have
That what you say is true

He really had me puzzled
What was I to do
I wanted him to stop
But I wanted to stay on the team too

It soon became a part
Of my daily prayer
That the LORD would protect me
And keep me in HIS care

Things began to get much better
And soon the coach moved away
The people I told about him
Believed what I had to say

But he took along with him
The things that happened in our town
No longer would innocent children
Have to have him around

The words my mother taught me
Seemed to come through the air
Take your troubles and your burdens
To the LORD in prayer

Mother

WHO IS A MOTHER

A mother is the woman
Who loves and cares for you
A mother is the woman
Who will always see you through

She's the one who cleaned your bottom
And cleaned up all your mess
She's the one who calmed your fears
As you snuggled to her breast

Mom's the one who was up with you
Often throughout the night
To check on your fever, read a book
Or tuck you in real tight

She's the one who, as we grew older
And we stepped across the line
We often went to bed
Without a chance to dine

The spankings, switchings and punishments
Were for our own good
She wanted us to be obedient and respectful
As a well-trained child should

Mom didn't tolerate backtalk
Lies, stealing or any deceit
If you got to big for your britches
A backhand might knock you off your feet

There are changes today for some of us
In the way we train-up a child
The way some children are ending up
I feel the parenting may be too mild

As we grew older and tried many things
Some not always for our best
Mother was there to see us through
And she suffered through these tests

She did her very best
To bring us up in the love of GOD
She certainly believed, to have spoiled a child
You must have spared the rod

She helped put food on the table
And clothes on our back
She did all that she could
To see that we didn't suffer or lack

We didn't need to have the most expensive clothes
What we had Mom kept clean and neat
Her love and caring was worth so much more
It was a combination that couldn't be beat

At times our actions may have
Caused her tears and pain
All of her talks, time and energy
Were spent for our gain

Maybe we didn't get
All the things we thought we needed
Even after we cried, begged
Or got on our knees and pleaded

She wanted the best for us
An education and a decent life
To treat others with the love of GOD
And not be burdened with worry and strife

As a mother ages, and isn't able
To do quite as much
Never forget her love
Or her motherly touch

She may become frail and sickly
As she is blessed to get on in years
Be kind, patient and loving
Wipe her tears and soother her fears

Always let your mother know
How dear she is to you
How much you appreciate all she did
To love, protect, train and take good care of you

Any woman can be a mother
She didn't have to born you into this world
A mother becomes a mother when she accepts you
To love and cherish as her own boy or girl

If your relationship with your mom
Isn't all that it should be
Get started today, to set things right
And do it with all your might

Ask GOD to intervene
To heal pains from the past
Because love, peace and harmony
Are what you want to last

If your mom has gone home
To her eternal rest
Hold close your memories
They'll be some of your best

A GODLY MOTHER

Was Momma sweet
Was Momma nice
When Momma called
Did she have to call twice

But you remember
That once was all it took
Because you were raised by the hand
And not by the book

You weren't abused
But you didn't run wild
Momma knew the best way
To raise a well-mannered child

She did it with a firm hand
But with plenty of love
Because Momma had strong faith
In the LORD above

She made sacrifices
To give you what you needed
And her guidance in your life
Had best be heeded

We weren't by any means rich
But GOD always provided and made a way
We were rich in love and togetherness
And that love still holds true to this day

Sunday school and church
Were regular parts of life in our home
Even as an adult,
From GOD's teachings you didn't roam

Momma did and said her best
To teach us to keep GOD as the head of our lives
So that one day we too
Would be Godly husbands and wives

We don't see each other every day
But really we don't have to
The love my brothers and I share
Is love that is heartfelt and true

Momma has gone home to the LORD
But the lessons still live in my heart
Because of her love and teachings
From CHRIST I will not depart

Resurrection

HE AROSE

HE arose that glorious morning
HE was no longer in the grave
HE arose that glorious morning
So that you and I would be saved

HE suffered pain and rejection
The FATHER had turned HIS face away
HE arose that glorious morning
In the grave HE could not stay

JESUS took all of our sins upon HIMSELF
HE didn't have to die that day
All HE had to do was call the angels
They would have kept all harm away

But HE didn't come down
HE stayed on the cross
HE suffered and died for us
So that we wouldn't be lost

HE did no harm
HE knew no sin
HE wanted us to have eternal life
And HIS peace and joy within

So celebrate that joyous morning
That our SAVIOUR rose from the grave
Celebrate the victory
And thank GOD that you're saved

WHAT HE DID FOR US

HE took all of our sins upon HIMSELF
HE suffered rejection, denial and pain
HE endured it for all of us
So that heaven would be our gain

HE was lied on and beat
HE was spit on and suffered much
Through all of HIS suffering
HE never received a comforting touch

HE carried that heavy cross
HE endured crucifixion for you and me
HE laid down HIS life
So that from sin we would be set free

HE arose that third day morning
With victory over sin, death and the grave
HE did it for all of us
So that you and I might be saved

HE didn't have to suffer
HE didn't have to die
But to save all of us
That is the reason why

HE took all of our sins
In time past, time present and time to be
What a wonderful, loving SAVIOUR
Thank you, LORD, for all that you did for me

Printed in the United States
31115LVS00001B/91